student WORKBOOK

AQA (A)

GW00337575

AS Psychology
Physiological Psychology & Individual Differences
Molly Marshall

Philip Allan Updates
Market Place, Deddington, Oxfordshire OX15 0SE
tel: 01869 338652, fax: 01869 337590
e-mail: sales@philipallan.co.uk
www.philipallan.co.uk

© Philip Allan Updates 2005

ISBN 1 84489 116 X

Printed by Raithby, Lawrence & Co. Ltd, Leicester

Environmental information
The paper on which this title is printed is sourced from managed, sustainable forests.

P00395

Introduction

The aim of this workbook is to help you increase your understanding of physiological psychology and individual differences and to improve your skills in answering the types of question you might encounter in the AQA (A) AS examination.

The workbook includes a variety of stimulus material that will help you to learn about psychological research, terminology and concepts. The questions are wide-ranging and designed to support you as you develop skills of analysis, interpretation and evaluation. Writing answers to the questions will help you learn to communicate your knowledge and understanding of psychology in a clear and effective manner. The questions are organised so that they become progressively more difficult within each topic. As you complete the workbook, you should become confident that you are learning the content required for the exam and how to write effective answers that will achieve high marks.

The workbook follows the AQA (A) specification. It is organised into two sections.

Section 1 Physiological psychology
This section comprises four topics. Topic 1 focuses on the body's response to stressors, including the general adaptation syndrome (Selye). Topic 2 examines research into the relationship between stress and physical illness, including cardiovascular disorders and the effects of stress on the immune system. Topic 3 looks at the sources of stress, including life changes (as measured on the Holmes and Rahe social readjustment rating scale) and workplace stressors (e.g. work overload, role ambiguity). Topic 4 focuses on methods of managing the negative effects of stress, including physiological treatments (e.g. drugs, biofeedback) and psychological approaches (e.g. Meichenbaum on stress inoculation and Kobasa on increasing hardiness).

Section 2 Individual differences
This section comprises three topics. Topic 1 deals with attempts to define psychological abnormality and their limitations. Topic 2 looks at biological and psychological models of abnormality. Topic 3 looks at the clinical characteristics of anorexia nervosa and bulimia nervosa and the explanations of these disorders in terms of biological and psychological models of abnormality.

You can study either Section 1 or Section 2 of this workbook first. To gain maximum benefit, you should complete the topics and questions in the order given within each section. There are several ways in which you can use this workbook:

(1) As an integral part of your learning experience, in conjunction with your class notes, handouts and textbook. Periodically, your teacher might ask you to hand your book in for assessment.
(2) As a revision tool, in which case you should work through the topics, writing the answers as practice for the exam.
(3) As a combination of **(1)** and **(2)**: if, as you progress through the module, you write answers to all the questions in this book, at the end of the course you will have created a valuable resource from which to revise!

Whichever way you choose, I hope the workbook will help you in your studies and in your exam.

Topic 1 Stress as a bodily response

I expect you know what it feels like to be stressed. Perhaps you have experienced stress before an exam when your heart beats faster and your palms start to sweat. In this topic, you will learn how psychologists explain the physiology (the bodily responses) of stress. Physiological psychology focuses on biological explanations of behaviour, such as how and why the brain and nervous system respond to stressors.

Item 1
What is stress?

Stress is a type of alarm reaction, involving heightened mental and bodily states. It is both a psychological and a physiological response to the environment. Your brain produces a stress reaction when you are in a situation that is physically or mentally demanding. **Stress is normal** and some stress is good for you — it keeps you alert and protects you in times of danger or when you need to act or think quickly. Physical fitness training places stress on your body, but that stress has a beneficial effect. Feeling a bit stressed about exams is normal — it may help you to focus your energy on revising well. However, prolonged and unwanted stress may lead to mental and physical health problems.

When psychologists talk about 'stress', they may refer to the **causes** of stress reactions (stressors) or to the **effects** of stress reactions on our physical and mental functioning. Stress can

be explained as a stimulus in the environment that causes a stress response. For example, if you worry about exams, a forthcoming exam could be defined as a 'stressor', and your rapid heart rate and sweating palms before the exam could be explained as the 'stress response'.

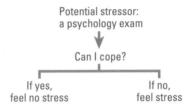

Of course, not everyone worries about exams. Thus, stress can be defined as the response that happens when **we think we cannot cope** with a stressor in the environment. If we think we cannot cope, we feel stress and when we feel stress, we experience physiological changes.

Item 2
The hypothalamic–pituitary–adrenal axis

The stress response originates in the hypothalamus and includes the pituitary and adrenal glands. This hypothalamic–pituitary–adrenal axis is responsible for arousing the autonomic nervous system (ANS) in response to a stressor.

Under stress, the sympathetic branch of the nervous system stimulates the adrenal gland to release adrenaline, noradrenaline and corticosteroids into the bloodstream. This produces the physiological reactions, such as increased heart rate and blood pressure and a dry mouth, known as the 'fight or flight' response.

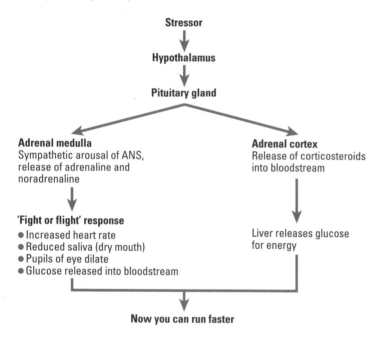

Item 3
The general adaptation syndrome (GAS)

Selye (1956) proposed that stress leads to a depletion of the body's resources, leaving the animal vulnerable to illness. He used the word 'stress' to describe the fact that many different stimuli (fear, pain, injury) all produce the same response. He called these 'stressors' and proposed that the body reacts in the same general way to all these stressors by producing a response which helps the animal adapt to the stressors and continue to function. Selye called this the 'general adaptation syndrome' (GAS) and identified three stages in the model.

1 **Alarm** When we perceive a stressor, the ANS responds. Adrenaline, noradrenaline and corticosteroids (hormones) are released into the bloodstream. The bodily reaction is increased arousal levels in readiness for a physical response (fight or flight), i.e. the heart rate increases, blood pressure rises and muscles tense.

2 **Resistance** If the stressor continues, the bodily reaction (the fight or flight response) ceases and we appear to be coping. But output from the adrenal cortex continues and the adrenal glands may become enlarged.

3 **Exhaustion** If the stressor continues for a long time, the body is unable to cope. The body's resources are reduced but alarm signs, such as increased blood pressure, may return. The person may become depressed and unable to concentrate. The immune system may be damaged and stress-related diseases, such as stomach ulcers, high blood pressure and depression, are more likely to occur.

Item 4
Mary and Jim have a stressful day

It was a fine sunny day and Mary was pushing her new baby in his buggy in the park. As she rounded the corner by the paddling pool, a huge dog rushed towards her growling and barking. She was terrified of dogs and in a panic she started to run.

Jim woke up with a sinking feeling in his chest. He had failed to win the new client and his manager was not going to be pleased. As he dressed he switched on the radio and heard there was a 20-mile traffic jam on the M25. Now he would be late again. He hated his job, and had done for months. He threw his clothes on and, hearing the telephone ring, he swore and ran downstairs.

Topic 1 Stress as a bodily response

Answers

1 Read your textbook and Item 1. Complete the following sentences.
a A stressor is…
b Stress can be defined as…

1a The thing causing cause of the stress reaction

b The reaction to the stressor, eg heightened mental bodily state preparing you for 'fight/flight'

2 Read your textbook and Item 2. Use the words in the list below to fill in the blanks in this description of the hypothalamic–pituitary–adrenal axis.
- dilated
- mouth
- pituitary
- hypothalamus
- physiological
- gland
- bloodstream
- adrenal
- adrenaline

2 The stress response originates in the _hypothalamus_ and includes the _adrenal_ and _pituitary_ glands. This hypothalamic–pituitary–adrenal axis is responsible for arousing the autonomic nervous system (ANS) in response to a stressor. When under stress, the sympathetic branch of the nervous system stimulates the adrenal _gland_ to release _adrenaline_, noradrenaline and corticosteroids into the _bloodstream_. This produces the _physiological_ reactions, such as increased heart rate and blood pressure, _dilated_ pupils and dry _mouth_, known as the 'fight or flight' response.

3 Read Item 2. Reorder these sentences so that they represent the correct sequence of the hypothalamic–pituitary–adrenal axis.

3
_3_ The ANS is activated.

_5_ The pituitary gland releases adrenocorticotrophic hormone into the bloodstream.

_2_ A signal is sent to the hypothalamus.

_7_ This stimulates the adrenal cortex to release corticosteroids.

_6_ This stimulates the adrenal medulla to release adrenaline and noradrenaline.

_4_ A message is sent to the pituitary gland.

_1_ The evaluation of a stressor occurs in the cerebral cortex.

_8_ This leads to an increase in heart rate and blood pressure.

_8_

4 Read your textbook and Item 3. Complete the right-hand column of the table to produce a model of Selye's GAS.

	Description of Selye's GAS
Stage 1	Alarm - body registers stressor, surge of ACTH, adrenaline, noradrenaline + corticosteroids
Stage 2	Resistance - body appears to be coping
Stage 3	Exhaustion - body becomes exhausted
Reasons for link between stress and illness	
Strength(s)	
Weakness(es)	
Conclusion	

5 Read Item 4.

   a Referring to Selye's GAS, explain which stage of the syndrome Mary may be in, the physiology of what is happening to Mary and why it is happening.

5a

   b Now explain which stage of the syndrome Jim may be in, and the possible threats to his health.

b

6 Read your textbook and Items 1, 2 and 3. Selye's GAS can be described as a 'reductionist' model. Explain why.

6

Stress and cardiovascular disorders

Item 1
Cardiovascular disorders

Cardiovascular disorders are disorders of the heart and blood vessels and are sometimes linked with stress. People who experience stress may engage in unhealthy activities, such as smoking and drinking alcohol in an attempt to relieve the stress. These behaviours increase the likelihood that the person may develop a cardiovascular disorder, so stress may cause illness indirectly.

Long-term stress may also have a direct effect on the cardiovascular system. Stress causes high heart rate and high blood pressure. Long-term stress can damage blood vessels because adrenaline and noradrenaline contribute to increases in blood cholesterol levels, leading to blood clots and thickened arteries. Weakened or damaged blood vessels may cause haemorrhages which in turn may lead to blockages in blood vessels, causing strokes or heart attacks.

Item 2
Research into the effect of stress on blood flow (Krantz et al. 1991)

In this study, the direct effect of stress on blood flow and blood pressure was investigated. Thirty-nine participants performed a stress-inducing task (e.g. a maths test) while their blood pressure and rate of blood flow to the heart was measured. The stressful task caused a reduced blood flow to the heart and led to raised blood pressure. From this it was concluded that stress does have a direct effect on the cardiovascular system, making cardiovascular disorders more likely.

Item 3
Friedman and Rosenman (1974)

Cardiologists Friedman and Rosenman defined two types of behaviour pattern, Type A and Type B:

- **Type A behaviour.** Type A people move, walk, eat and talk rapidly, and try to do two or more things at one time. In personality, Type A people are competitive and tend to judge themselves by the number of successes they have rather than the quality of their successes. Type A individuals are hard-driving, impatient and aggressive. They tend to be achievement-oriented and hostile. In physiology, Type A people have a higher level of cholesterol and fat in their bloodstream, have a more difficult time getting the cholesterol out of their bloodstream, and have a greater likelihood of clotting within the arteries.
- **Type B behaviour.** Type B people seldom feel any sense of time urgency or impatience, are not preoccupied with their achievements or accomplishments and seldom become angry or irritable. They tend to enjoy their recreation, are free of guilt about relaxing, and they work calmly and smoothly.

Aims Based on their observations of patients who displayed the common Type A behaviour pattern of impatience, competitiveness and hostility, Friedman and Rosenman aimed to test their belief that Type A personalities were more prone to coronary heart disease (CHD) than Type B personalities.

Procedures The sample comprised 3000 male volunteers, all from California, USA, aged between 39 and 59, who were healthy at the start of the study. Personality type was established through the use of a structured interview and observations of the participants' behaviour during the interview. The interviewer interrupted the interview from time to time to deliberately annoy Type A individuals. The answers to questions and behavioural responses were used to assess participants' impatience, competitiveness and hostility.

Findings Eight and a half years later, 257 of the men in the sample were diagnosed as having CHD. Seventy percent of those with CHD had been classified as Type A.

The Type A men were also found to have higher levels of adrenaline and cholesterol. Twice as many Type A men had died as compared with Type Bs. Type As also had higher blood pressure, higher cholesterol and other symptoms of CHD. Type As were more likely to smoke and have a family history of CHD, both of which would increase their risk.

Conclusion Type A personality is associated with illness and symptoms of CHD. Because Type A is also linked to other factors that cause CHD, such as smoking, it is not certain whether Type A is a direct or an indirect cause of CHD.

Criticisms
- This was a long-term study with a large sample having a baseline measure (all the men were free of CHD at the start of the study).
- The study showed how psychological factors (personality) are related to physiological factors (CHD).
- The study cannot show that Type A personality causes CHD. It may be that Type A behaviours develop as a result of long-term stress.
- Categorising all men into two personality types is reductionist. Later research has identified Type C and D personalities.
- The sample was both ethnocentric and gender biased (all males from the USA) and as such cannot be generalised to females.

The findings of **Williams (2000)** support Friedman and Rosenman in their description of Type A personalities as hostile. In the Williams' study, 13 000 participants completed questionnaires asking about their feelings of anger, and the participants' responses were rated for anger scores. Six years later, those with high anger scores were significantly more likely to have suffered a heart attack.

Stress and the immune system
Item 4
The immune system

The immune system comprises billions of cells that travel through the bloodstream. They are produced in the bone marrow, spleen, lymph nodes and thymus. The major type of immune cells is white blood cells which defend the body against antigens — bacteria, viruses and cancerous cells. Some types of immune cells produce antibodies that destroy antigens.

When we are stressed, the ability of the immune system to protect us against antigens is reduced, leading to an increased likelihood of physical illness. This weakening of the immune system is called the '**immunosuppressive effect of stress**'. In long-term stress, such as stage 3 of Selye's GAS, increased levels of corticosteroids can reduce the production of antibodies (a direct effect).

Item 5
Kiecolt-Glaser et al. (1984): stress and the immune system

Based on the assumption that the body's response to stress reduces the effectiveness of the immune system (immunosuppression), Kiecolt-Glaser et al. aimed to establish a link between stress and reduced immune system functioning.

Aims To look for evidence of a difference in immune response in high and low-stress conditions, and to see whether factors such as anxiety were associated with immune system functioning.

Procedures Seventy-five first-year medical students (49 male and 26 female) volunteered to give blood samples 1 month before their final exams, and after they had sat two papers on the first day of the exams. The blood samples

were analysed for how much 'natural killer cell' activity was present (natural killer cells help to protect against viruses). The students also completed questionnaires to assess symptoms of depression and loneliness, and to find out what other stressful events they might be experiencing.

Findings In comparison with the first blood sample, natural killer cell activity was significantly reduced in the second sample. It was most reduced in those students who were experiencing other stressful events, and in those who reported feeling anxious and depressed.

Conclusion Stress has an immunosuppressant effect and can be associated with reduced immune system function.

Criticisms
- The study has high mundane realism as the exams were real-life experiences and would have happened anyway.
- The first blood sample acted as a baseline control and the participants were being compared against themselves — this controlled for the effects of personality variables.
- It is not possible to say that no other variable could have caused the change in the students' immune systems as other variables could not be controlled (e.g. it might have been lack of sleep due to long hours revising that affected the immune system).
- It is not possible to say how long-lasting the reduced effectiveness of the immune system might be.

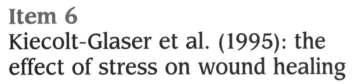

Item 6
Kiecolt-Glaser et al. (1995): the effect of stress on wound healing

The immune system is involved in helping the body repair itself after injury. Following tissue damage (cuts and wounds), the immune system produces interleukin B that promotes healing by helping to create scar tissue.

Aim To show that stress has an indirect effect on wound healing due to reduced effectiveness of the immune system.

Procedures The study involved 13 women who cared for relatives suffering from Alzheimer's disease (the high-stress group), and a control group of 13 women who had no stressful responsibilities (the no-stress group). All the women gave skin samples which caused skin wounds.

Findings The wounds of the carers in the high-stress group took, on average, 9 days longer than those of the no-stress group to heal. It was concluded that long-term stress reduces the effectiveness of the immune system to heal wounds.

Criticisms
- The study is useful to NHS staff as it may explain why the wounds of some patients take longer to heal than expected.
- The sample was small and all female, and it may not be safe to generalise the findings to other populations.
- There was no baseline measure of how rapidly the wounds might have healed in the high-stress group before the onset of the stressor.

Item 7
Can you help Dr Jamadi?

Dr Jamadi is baffled. Pansy and Dahlia are two of his elderly patients. He has been treating them for ulcers on their legs. Ulcers are difficult to treat and he has been very careful. Over the past 2 weeks, both women, whose ulcers are similar, have received the same treatment. In the case of Pansy, the ulcers are responding to treatment and are improving. In the case of Dahlia, the ulcer shows little sign of improvement. He is worried about Dahlia who, following her recent bereavement, seems to be depressed and anxious.

1 Read your textbook and Items 1 and 2.
  a Explain what is meant by 'cardiovascular disorders'.
  b Outline *one* way in which stress may be an indirect cause of cardiovascular disorders.
  c Outline *one* way in which stress may be a direct cause of cardiovascular disorders.

2 Read your textbook and Item 3. Write a synopsis of the aims, procedures, findings and conclusions of the research described in Item 3.

3 Read your textbook and Item 3. List *three* criticisms of research that conclude that stress may be related to cardiovascular disorders.

1a

b

c

2 Aims

Procedures

Findings

Conclusions

3

Topic 2 Stress and physical illness

4 Read your textbook and Item 4.

  a Outline what is meant by the 'immune system'.

4a

  b Explain how stress may reduce the effectiveness of the immune system.

b

  c What does 'stress is an immuno-suppressant' mean?

c

5 Read your textbook and Item 5. Outline the aims, procedures, findings and conclusions of the study of the relationship between stress and the immune system described in Item 5.

5 Aims

Procedures

Findings

Conclusions

6 Read Items 5 and 6. Outline *two* criticisms of research into the relationship between stress and the immune system.

6

7 Read your textbook and Items 5, 6 and 7. From what you know about Pansy and Dahlia, and from what you have learned about research into the relationship between stress and the immune system, write a letter to Dr Jamadi (quoting research evidence) to explain why Dahlia's ulcer may take longer to heal than Pansy's.

7

8 *Exam practice*

Review the items on stress and physical illness. To what extent has psychological research demonstrated a link between stress and physical illness?

a Write a list of points as an outline plan for this essay.

b In the exam you should, in about 100 words, describe appropriate psychological evidence (AO1 skills), and then provide about 200 words of evaluative commentary (AO2 skills).

c Try to use one of these phrases for each evaluation point you list:
- One strength of this research is…
- On the other hand…
- This implies that…
- This is useful because…
- Not all psychologists agree, for example…
- There are advantages to X because…
- These findings are reliable/ unreliable because…

d In your outline, identify the psychological evidence you will use and the evaluative points you will need.

Topic 3 Sources of stress

Life seems to be stressful much of the time, and there are many sources of stress — traffic jams, long queues at the supermarket, crying babies, too many exams (you could make your own list). But perhaps the two major sources of stress are work and changes in an individual's life.

- **Life events.** Throughout our lives we experience many changes, such as leaving home, going to university, marriage, changing employment, the birth of children and moving house. These events cause us to change the way we live, and adjusting to change may cause stress.
- **The workplace.** Going to work can be stressful. For some people, the kind of work they do, where they work and with whom they work can be a source of stress. Some of the more stressful occupations are nursing, teaching, social work and the emergency services. Someone who is stressed at work may become ill and need to take time off. Employers are concerned about stress at work because productivity is reduced when employees suffer from stress-related illness.

Understanding stress would be easy if we all responded to similar stressors in the same way. But, of course, we do not. Some people seem to thrive on lifestyles that others would find very stressful. In this topic, you will learn about the sources of stress and what psychologists know about individual differences in responding to stressors.

Life events

Item 1
Holmes and Rahe (1967): social readjustment rating scale (SRRS)

Aims (i) To construct an instrument for measuring stress (stress was defined as the amount of life changes people had experienced during a fixed period).
(ii) To show that the amount of life changes (i.e. the amount of stress) is related to psychological and physiological illness.

Procedures The medical records of 5000 patients were examined and a list was compiled of the 43 life events that appeared in the 12 months before their illnesses. One hundred people (the 'judges') were told that the life event of marriage had been rated at 500 points. They were then asked to rate how much readjustment each of the 43 life events would require 'relative to marriage'.

Findings (i) Death of a spouse was thought to require twice as much adjustment as marriage and was rated at 1000 points by the judges. The average for each of the 43 life events was calculated. Holmes and Rahe could now rank the 43 life events from death of a spouse (at 100 points) to minor violations of the law (11 points). A questionnaire was designed in which participants ticked the life events

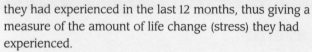

they had experienced in the last 12 months, thus giving a measure of the amount of life change (stress) they had experienced.

(ii) People with high scores on the SRRS (over the previous 12 months) were likely to experience some physical illness. A person having 300 points over 12 months had an 80% chance of becoming ill, and illnesses ranged from heart attacks to diabetes and sports injuries.

Conclusions (i) Stress can be objectively measured by the SRRS as a life changes score.

(ii) High scores on the SRRS (high-stress scores) predict physical illness, and stressful life changes cause physical illness.

Criticisms
- The research provides an objective measure of the relationship between stress and illness. Supporting evidence was found from a study in which 2500 navy personnel completed the SRRS before they left for a 6-month trip on board their ships. Health records were kept which found that high scores on the SRRS were correlated with physical illness.
- The experience of a life event is different for each person — for example, some people may be distressed by divorce whereas others are relieved. Life events other than the 43 on the SRRS may also cause stress, for example having your home flooded. In addition, most of the 43 life events are infrequent and the daily small hassles of life may be a more significant cause of stress.

Item 2
Hassles and stress

DeLongis et al. (1982) theorised that it was everyday hassles that caused stress. They created a hassles scale to assess the effect of the routine problems of life, such as getting stuck in a traffic jam. The hassles scale measures positive events (uplifts) as well as hassles. In people over 45, they found that the hassles scale was a better predictor of ill health than the SRRS. The frequency and intensity of hassles significantly correlated to ill health.

The workplace
Item 3
Stress in the workplace can originate in six areas

1 **Interpersonal factors.** Relationships with bosses, colleagues and customers may be stressful. Social support is very important in moderating the effects of stress in general. Good relationships with co-workers can reduce stress in the workplace; poor relationships at work can exacerbate stress.
2 **Work pressure.** Having too much work to do and working to strict deadlines can cause stress.
3 **The physical environment.** This may be noisy, hot and overcrowded, or may involve health risks and unsociable hours, such as working night shifts. Czeisler et al. (1982) researched the causes of health problems and sleep difficulties experienced by employees of a chemical plant in Utah, USA. The employees worked shifts. He recommended that

the pattern of shifts should be changed to a 21-day shift rotation and always 'shift forward' (phase advance). After 9 months, job satisfaction and productivity increased.

4 **Role stress.** Worry about job security or responsibility may cause stress.

5 **Role conflict.** Having to express one emotion while feeling another may cause stress, e.g. doctors, nurses, police.

6 **Control.** How much control people have over how they do a job may be a factor in how stressful the job is perceived to be.

Item 4
Johnson and Hall (1988): the importance of control and interpersonal relationships at work

Aim To investigate the relationship between variables in the workplace (social support, perceived control and how demanding jobs are) and the incidence of cardiovascular disease.

Procedures Data from 14 000 male and female Swedish workers were analysed to explore the relationship between cardiovascular disease and job stress, specifically stress associated with control, demand and social support. The data included four scales of measurement:

1 Work control, based on questions about the level of influence over the planning of work.

2 Work-related social support, based on questions about how and when workers could interact with co-workers.

3 Psychological demands of work, based on questions about how demanding the work was.

4 An indicator of cardiovascular health.

Findings
- Jobs that were perceived to be demanding but that involved low levels of control were related to increased incidences of heart disease.
- Where workers had fewer social interaction opportunities (low social support), there was an increase in cardio-vascular disease in the high demand, high control combination.
- Low social support combined with low control increased cardiovascular disease.

Conclusion Both social support and control are important factors in work-related stress.

Criticisms
- This research shows how factors such as control and social support at work are important in understanding workplace stress.
- Self-reports may result in inaccurate descriptions of job characteristics and may be biased by personality characteristics.
- Workplaces are complex. Using objective measures of workplace stress may result in a reductionist approach that overemphasises the social context of stress. Qualitative research is required in order to understand the meaning of events for individuals.

- This study was correlational. Thus it cannot be said that stress was the cause of physical illness. There are sources of stress outside the work environment, such as poor living conditions, and it is possible that the association found between job stress and illness was caused by other factors. For example, workers in low-paid jobs may experience a lack of control and noisy work environments but are also more likely to have poorer living conditions.

Item 5
Factors that may cause stress in the workplace

Role conflict in the workplace

Margolis and Kroes (1974) found that when the demands of the organisation conflict with the needs of the workers, stress may result. They found that when the job requires workers to express one emotion, e.g. being calm and cheerful, while really feeling another emotion, e.g. being unhappy or worried, this causes role conflict. Nurses, teachers and paramedics are likely to suffer stress caused by role conflict.

Is having control at work important?

Marmot et al. (1997) investigated whether perceived control is an important factor in work-related stress. In their study, 7000 civil service employees who worked in London partici-

pated in a survey. Data were gathered on how senior they were (their employment grade) and how much control and support they perceived they had at work. Five years later, the medical histories of the employees were reviewed. The participants who were less senior (lower grades) and who felt they had less control and less social support were more likely to have cardiovascular disorders. It was concluded that how much control people have at work, and how much social support people receive from colleagues, may be factors in whether they suffer from stress-related illness.

Item 6
Nelson's stressful life

Nelson is a gunner with a tank crew. He has just been promoted to sergeant. This led to his family being relocated to Germany, so they moved house. They moved twice last year. They used to be a happy family but now his teenage daughter hates her new school and blames him because she has no friends. His wife is miserable in Germany and she dislikes their new house. He is due to leave for a 6-month tour of duty in Iraq and is anxious about leaving his family. He and his wife row all the time, he feels guilty and he cannot sleep at night. On top of all his worries, he has started to make mistakes. Yesterday, he missed his practice target three times and the tank commander bawled him out in front of the whole crew. Still, he and his mates had a good laugh about that afterwards.

Individual differences in responses to stressors

Item 7
Personality differences and stress

The **Type A personality**, especially the hostile Type A personality, is significantly associated with coronary heart disease. The **Type C personality**, hardworking, conventional and sociable, responds to stress with a sense of helplessness and may be more likely to suffer from cancer. In support of this, **Morris et al. (1981)** found a link between people who tended to suppress their anger and the increased incidence of cancer.

Helgeson and Fritz (1999) studied nearly 300 patients receiving treatment for blocked arteries. Six months later, they found that those patients who were lowest in 'cognitive adaptation' were three times more likely to have experienced a new coronary event. High cognitive adaptation included an ability to develop a positive outlook about one's medical condition and a sense of control in most situations. They concluded that the 'pessimist personality' is more likely to become ill as a result of stress.

Kobasa (1979) proposed that some people are better able to deal with stress (the hardy personality) and that all people could learn to behave in this way in order to cope better. The key traits of a hardy personality, known as the three Cs, are having a strong sense of personal *control*, a strong sense of purpose (*commitment*) and the ability to see problems positively, as *challenges* to be overcome rather than as stressors.

Item 8
Gender differences and stress

More men suffer from coronary heart disease than women and there are several explanations as to why gender may be an important factor in stress:
- women are biologically more able to cope with stress
- women are socialised to cope better with stress
- women tend to drink and smoke less and may do less stressful work

From an **evolutionary (biological) perspective**, men should respond to situations of danger with the 'fight or flight' arousal response, whereas women should respond by looking after young ones and each other. **Taylor et al. (2000)** reviewed many biological and behavioural studies (both human and animal) and concluded that females were more likely to deal with stress by nurturing those around them and reaching out to others. Men were more likely to hide away or start a confrontation. This suggests different responses to stress which match gender types.

From a **social perspective**, males and females are socialised in different ways. Women learn to use social networks more and this may reduce their stress. Women are taught to think about social conflict situations differently. **Vögele et al. (1997)** proposed that females learn to control their anger and react more calmly in stressful situations, but males learn that anger is an acceptable response and feel stress if they have to suppress anger. **Iso et al. (2002)** looked at 73 000 white Japanese participants aged 40–79. Participants were asked to rate the level of stress in their daily lives. Over the following 8 years, those Japanese women who reported high levels of mental stress were more than twice as likely to die from stroke and heart disease than women reporting low stress levels.

There may also be **gender differences in lifestyles**. Women engage in fewer unhealthy behaviours than men, e.g. they smoke and drink less. Perhaps the Western stereotype that 'men do not talk about their feelings' leads men to resort to drinking and smoking as a way of coping with stress.

Item 9
Culture and stress

There are observed differences in rates of coronary heart disease between different racial or cultural groups. Most notably black Americans are more likely to have cardiovascular disorders than white Americans. There may be several explanations for this.

- **Biological.** It is unlikely that, within the same species, differences are biological. One study (Cooper et al. 1999) compared hypertension rates of Africans living in Western cities with Africans living in rural Africa. Hypertension rates were highest in urban societies. This suggests that hypertension is due to social factors and not to race. However, race should not be confused with culture. Culture is a social concept, though many cultures contain people who are racially similar.

- **Socialisation.** Cultural differences in coping with stress may be due to different social practices. For example, life

spans vary from one cultural group to another. The Abraskian people from what was part of Russia have 100 times greater frequency of living to ages over 100 than people in the UK (Weg 1983). This suggests they cope better with life stressors. This may be partly due to biological factors but is also related to factors such as dietary habits, amount of physical activity, lack of stress and good social support. It may be that coping strategies for stress are culturally determined and thus culture may be an important factor in modifying stress.

- **Other factors.** Cultural differences may correlate with other factors, such as poor living conditions and more stress from experiencing prejudice. Black Americans are likely to experience more stress in their lives because of prejudice and because they are more likely to be in the lower social classes. This could explain why they are more likely to have cardiovascular problems than their white counterparts.

Item 10
A stressful time

Matthew had a hangover. He had been out with his mates the night before and had drunk far too much. He hardly heard his tutor droning on about revision and planning. He dreaded the weeks to come. In just 2 weeks time he had to sit 10 exams. To get into his first-choice university, he needed an A and two Bs and he was worried he wouldn't make the grades. His notes were in a muddle and he could feel the tension building up. He glanced around and wondered whether his classmates all felt as desperate and as stressed as he did.

1 Read your textbook and Item 1. Explain what psychologists mean when they write about 'life change events' and give *two* examples.

2 Read your textbook and Items 1 and 2.
   a In your own words, explain the difference between a 'life change event' and a 'hassle'.

   b Explain what psychologists mean by an 'uplift'.

   c Describe the aims, procedures, findings, conclusions and *two* criticisms of *one* study of the relationship between life events and stress.

Answers

1

2a

b

c Aims

Procedures

Findings

Conclusions

Criticism 1

Criticism 2

Topic 3 Sources of stress

d Describe the findings and conclusions of *one* study of the relationship between daily hassles and stress.

d

3 Outline evidence that suggests that stress can be explained in terms of life changes and then list *three* criticisms of this evidence.

3 Evidence

Criticism 1

Criticism 2

Criticism 3

4 Read your textbook and Item 3.
  a What is meant by a 'workplace stressor'?

  b Item 3 describes several sources of stress in the workplace. Referring to these, outline *one* source of stress you would expect to be present in each of the jobs described here.

5 Read Items 4, 5 and 6. Much research into stress in the workplace involves interviewing people and asking them to complete questionnaires. Suggest *one* advantage and *one* disadvantage of using self-report methods to gather data on workplace stressors.

4a ....
....
....

  b Checkout operator in large supermarket
....

Cleaner in a large comprehensive school
....

Doctor in a busy town surgery
....

Staff nurse working nights in an accident and emergency department
....

Project manager on a North Sea oil-drilling platform
....

Volunteer worker in a charity shop
....

5 ....
....
....
....
....
....

Topic 3 Sources of stress

6 Read your textbook and Items 4, 5 and 6. Describe the aims, procedures, findings, conclusions and *two* criticisms of *one* study of workplace stressors.

6 Aims

Procedures

Findings

Conclusions

Criticism 1

Criticism 2

7 Read Item 4. You have just been appointed as manager of human resources in a factory that employs 500 people. The factory makes widgets and production is ongoing, 24 hours a day, 7 days each week. The factory has high levels of sickness and absenteeism. Based on the Johnson and Hall (1988) findings, describe *two* changes to factory procedures that you think may reduce these levels.

7

8 Review your notes and study Item 6.

a Make a list of all the stressors in Nelson's life. Based on what you know about Nelson, explain whether Holmes and Rahe would predict that he is likely to suffer a stress-related illness.

b Suggest whether DeLongis et al. would agree with Holmes and Rahe about Nelson. Give reasons for your suggestions.

8a

b

9 Read through Items 7, 8 and 9.

a Explain what psychologists mean by 'individual differences'.

b List *three* factors that modify stress.

c Describe *two* effects of personality on stress.

d Explain *one* way that gender may modify the effects of stressors.

e Outline *two* ways by which culture may modify the effects of stressors.

9a

b

c

d

e

10 Read Item 10. Write a letter to Matthew explaining the ways that individual differences modify the effects of stressors.

10

What do you do when you feel stressed? If you ask your friends and family to describe what they do, you will probably find they all do different things. Some people smoke and drink more. Some people eat more and some eat less. Some people sleep longer and some may not sleep at all. There are many ways of coping with stress and the effectiveness of the coping strategy depends on the type of stressor and the characteristics of the person who is trying to cope.

Item 1
Stress management

Stress management refers to therapies used by doctors in clinical situations and to coping strategies taught by psychologists. It can also refer to the informal ways in which people try to cope with stress in their lives. Psychologists categorise coping strategies as:
- physiological or psychological, and
- emotion-focused or problem-focused

Physiological approaches to stress management help people cope by changing the way the body responds to stress. They focus on the reduction of physical symptoms of stress.

Psychological approaches to stress management help people cope by getting them to think about their problems in a different way. Such approaches focus on encouraging people to deal with the causes of their stress. One psychological approach is to increase the sense of control people have in stressful situations.

Emotion-focused approaches may attempt to reduce the symptoms of anxiety by taking a physiological approach — for example, biofeedback or anti-anxiety drugs may be used.

Problem-focused approaches attempt to change how people respond to stressors, e.g. by using cognitive therapies or by encouraging people to increase their social support.

It is important to note that emotion-focused and problem-focused approaches are not exclusive categories, as problem-focused approaches also deal with emotions.

Item 2
Physiological approaches to stress management

Drugs
Drugs aim to reduce the physiological, or bodily, response to stress. Two drugs which do this are benzodiazepine and beta-blockers.

Benzodiazepine is an anti-anxiety drug and its brand names include Librium and Valium. These drugs slow down the activity of the central nervous system (CNS) and reduce anxiety by enhancing the activity of a natural biochemical substance, gamma-amino-butyric-acid (GABA). GABA is the body's natural form of anxiety relief and it also reduces **serotonin** activity. Serotonin is a neurotransmitter and people with anxiety need to reduce their levels of serotonin.

Beta-blockers act on the sympathetic nervous system (SNS) rather than the brain. They reduce heart rate and blood pressure and thus reduce the harmful effects of stress.

Advantages of drugs
- They are quick and effective and reduce the physiological effects of stress.
- People prefer drug therapies to psychological therapies because 'taking a pill is easy'.
- They do not require people to change the way they think or behave.
- They can be used in conjunction with psychological methods.

Limitations of drugs
- All drugs have side effects. Benzodiazepines can cause drowsiness and may affect memory.
- Long-term use of drugs can lead to physical and psychological dependency.
- They treat the symptoms of stress. Most stresses are psychological and drugs do not address the causes of the problem.

Biofeedback
Biofeedback works because our minds can influence the automatic functions of our bodies. Using a special machine, people can learn to control processes such as heart rate and blood pressure. Biofeedback machines provide information about the systems in the body that are affected by stress. The **electromyogram (EMG)** measures muscle tension. Electrodes are placed on your skin and when tension is detected, the machine gives you a signal. As you become aware of this internal process, you can learn techniques to control tension. **Galvanic skin response (GSR)** training devices measure electrical conductance in the skin. A tiny electrical current is run through your skin and the machine measures changes in sweat gland ducts. The more emotionally aroused (stressed) you are, the more active your sweat glands are, and the greater the electrical conductivity of your skin.

There are four stages in learning biofeedback:
- The person is attached to a machine that monitors changes in heart rate and blood pressure and gives feedback.
- The person learns to control the symptoms of stress by deep breathing and muscle relaxation; this slows down their heart rate, making them feel more relaxed.
- The biofeedback from the machine acts like a reward and encourages the person to repeat the breathing techniques.
- Through practice, the person learns to repeat the breathing techniques in stressful situations.

Advantages of biofeedback
- There are no side effects.
- It reduces symptoms and gives people a sense of control.
- The learned techniques can be generalised to other stressful situations.
- It is more effective if combined with psychological therapies that encourage people to think about the causes of their stress and how their behaviour may contribute to it.

Limitations of biofeedback

- It requires specialist equipment and expert supervision.
- It requires the stressed person to commit time and effort.
- Very anxious people may find learning biofeedback techniques difficult and it may not be effective therapy for children.

Item 3
Psychological approaches to stress management

Stress inoculation (Meichenbaum 1985)

The aim of this cognitive behavioural therapy is to prepare people to cope with stress in a similar way to which an injection prevents a disease. Training people to deal with stress before it becomes a problem involves three stages:

1 Conceptualisation — patients identify and express their feelings and fears. They are encouraged to imagine stressful situations and analyse what is stressful about them and how they might deal with them.

2 Skill acquisition and rehearsal — patients practise how to relax and how to express their emotions. Specific skills may be taught, such as positive thinking, communication skills and time-management.

3 Application and follow through — patients are supported through progressively more threatening real-life situations while applying the newly acquired skills.

Advantages of stress inoculation

- It focuses on the cause of stress and ways of coping with it.

- It is effective for both short- and long-term stressors and can be combined with other treatment methods.
- The increased feelings of 'being in control' and improved communication and time-management skills lead to increased self-confidence and self-efficacy.
- There are no physiological side effects.

Limitations of stress inoculation

- It may only be successful with patients who are already determined to make the time and effort to help themselves.
- The research findings are based on a narrow sample (mainly white middle-class, well-educated people); thus they may not generalise to other populations.

Increasing hardiness (Kobasa 1977)

The aim of increasing hardiness is to encourage people to respond to stressors in a positive manner instead of perceiving them as disasters, and to teach the behavioural, physiological and cognitive skills that enable them to cope with stressors. Hardiness training involves three stages:

1 Focusing — patients are taught to recognise the signs of stress, such as muscle tension and tiredness, and to identify the sources of the stress.

2 Re-living stressful encounters — patients are asked to re-live stressful situations and to analyse these situations so that they can learn from past experience.

3 Self-improvement — patients use the insights gained so that they see stressors as challenges that can be coped with, leading to improved self-confidence and an enhanced sense of personal control.

Advantages of increasing hardiness

- Evidence suggests this approach is effective. Williams et al. (1992) found that 'high' hardy people use more problem-focused and support-seeking measures when dealing with stress than 'low' hardy people who tend to use avoidance and wishful thinking. Hardiness is associated with successful coping strategies.
- As with stress inoculation, hardiness training focuses on coping with the causes of stress.
- It can be combined with other treatment methods and improves self-confidence and self-efficacy.

Limitations of increasing hardiness

- The research findings are based on an all male sample and may not generalise to females.
- It may only be successful with patients who see stress as a challenge to be coped with.
- The concept of hardiness is complex, and in very stressful situations even hardy personalities may succumb to anxiety and negative thinking.

Item 4
The role of control in stress management

Psychological research suggests that the role of control in managing stress is important. Having a sense of 'being in control' has been shown to reduce stress. Psychological approaches to stress management emphasise taking cognitive control, by thinking positively in order to minimise the effects of stressors.

Locus of control (Rotter 1966)

Rotter categorised people into two types. Those having an **external locus of control** believe that good things happen because of luck, and bad things happen because someone else causes them to. People having an external locus of control perceive they have no control and are likely to become anxious in stressful situations. Those having an **internal locus of control** see themselves as responsible for what happens to them and are more likely to take action to manage stressful situations.

The illusion of control (Glass and Singer 1972)

In this study, two groups of participants were exposed to loud noise. In the experimental condition, participants were deceived into believing they could control the noise by pressing a button. In the control condition, participants were simply exposed to loud noise. Galvanic skin response (GSR) was used to measure the stress response (arousal levels) of both groups. The experimental group which believed it had control showed lower arousal levels (reduced stress response). It was concluded that people who believe they are in control in stressful situations, even if they actually have no control, are less likely to become stressed.

Langer and Rodin (1976)

In a controlled study, residents in an old people's home were given more personal control over their lives. Those who had choices and who were able to make decisions were more active, happier and lived longer. Those who had no control were less active and less healthy.

Item 5
Hypothetical case studies

Ranjit is 38. For 2 years he has been working on a very large project that involves monthly travel between the UK, France and Spain and he is tired and stressed. He has been to his doctor who has told him that his blood pressure is significantly raised and that he is suffering from chronic stress.

Robert is 49. He works shifts and has just moved into a new flat. The students who live next door play loud music at all hours of the day and night. Robert feels anxious and stressed. Some days when the music starts he wonders how he can carry on. He doesn't feel he can take control of the situation by confronting the students and wonders whether his doctor can help.

Answers

1 Read your textbook and Items 1 and 2.

1a

a What is the meaning of the term 'stress management'?

b Outline what is meant by 'physiological approaches to stress management'.

b

c Outline what is meant by 'psychological approaches to stress management'.

c

d Outline what is meant by 'biofeedback'.

d

e Explain how biofeedback can be used in the physiological approach to stress management.
(**Hint:** be clear *why* biofeedback is a physiological approach.)

e

f Outline *one* advantage and *one* limitation of biofeedback as a method of stress management.

f

g Explain two advantages of using drugs to manage stress.
(**Hint:** don't forget to say why they *are* advantages, e.g. this is an advantage because…)

g

h Outline *two* limitations of using drug therapy as a method of stress management.
(**Hint:** don't forget to say why they *are* a limitation, e.g. this may be a problem because…)

h

2 Read your textbook and Item 3.

a Complete the table to show *two* differences between physiological and psychological approaches to stress management.

b Describe *one* psychological approach to stress management.

c Explain *two* reasons why psychological approaches to stress management may not always be effective.

d Explain *one* major advantage of using psychological approaches to manage stress.
(**Hint:** don't forget to explain why it is an advantage.)

2a

	Physiological approaches	Psychological approaches
1		
2		

b

c

d

Topic 4 Critical issue: stress management

3 Read your textbook and Items 1–4.

a As a revision exercise, fill in the blanks so that this passage makes sense. Some of the words and phrases are listed below.
- stress
- physiological
- biofeedback
- emotion-focused

b Explain what psychologists mean by 'control' in relation to stress management.

c Outline the conclusions of psychological research into the role of control in relation to stress.

3a Stress management refers to techniques used by doctors, therapists and individuals to try to manage .... Some psychologists distinguish between problem-focused and .... - .... coping strategies. .... approaches to managing stress include anti-anxiety drugs and .... Psychological approaches include .... (Meichenbaum) and .... hardiness (Kobasa). One of the three Cs in the concept of .... is .... Rotter categorised people as having either external or internal .... and theorised that people with an .... locus of control will .... more effectively as they are more likely to take action to reduce the stress.

b

c

4 Read Item 5. You are a clinical psychologist and have recently organised a stress-management clinic. Both Ranjit and Robert have been referred for help.

a Write a report to Ranjit explaining how chronic stress presents a risk to his physical health and suggesting what action he could take to reduce and manage his high levels of stress.

b Write a report for Robert's doctor outlining recommendations for a stress-management programme for Robert.

(**Hint:** Don't forget to cite the research from all four topics you have studied. Base your recommendations on the research, and outline what you expect the outcomes to be.)

4a

b

5 *Exam practice*

Review your notes and Items 1–4. Evaluate the extent to which psychological approaches to stress management (including the role of control) may be effective in reducing stress.

a Write a list of points as an outline plan for this essay.

b In the exam you should describe, in about 100 words, appropriate psychological evidence (AO1 skills), and then provide about 200 words of evaluative commentary (AO2 skills).

c Try to use one of these phrases for each evaluation point you list:
- One strength of this research is…
- On the other hand…
- This implies that…
- This is useful because…
- Not all psychologists agree, for example…
- There are advantages to X because…
- These findings are reliable/unreliable because…

d In your outline, identify the psychological evidence you will use and the evaluative points you will need.

You have already learned that people differ, and that behaviour may be affected by variables, such as gender, personality traits and social and cultural norms. So how can you decide whether a person is psychologically normal or abnormal? Some of the methods psychologists use include statistical infrequency, deviation from social norms, a failure to function adequately and deviation from ideal mental health. In this topic, you will learn about psychological approaches to defining abnormality and about the limitations associated with these definitions.

Item 1
Abnormality as behaviour which deviates from the statistical norm

Some psychologists propose that behaviour is normally distributed. If this is true, then people whose behaviour is very different (more than two standard deviations above or below the mean) can be defined as 'abnormal'. The diagram shows that people whose behaviour falls more than three standard deviations above the average will be very rare.

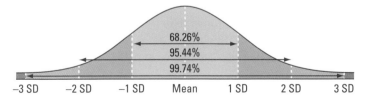

However, this statistical approach has limitations:

- It accounts for the frequency of behaviour, not its desirability. A very low IQ is, statistically, just as abnormal as a very high IQ, but it is desirable to have a high IQ. Therefore, frequency of behaviour tells us nothing about its desirability.
- It does not allow us to distinguish between rare behaviour that is eccentric (elective), such as keeping snails as pets, and rare behaviour that is psychologically abnormal, such as schizophrenia.
- It is difficult to define the point at which normal behaviour becomes abnormal behaviour. For example, at what point on the distribution curve does a person's IQ become abnormal?
- Some behaviour, such as depressive illness, is psychologically abnormal but is not that rare.

Item 2
Abnormality as behaviour which deviates from the social norm

Some people behave in socially deviant ways. Because their behaviour does not fit in with social norms or meet social expectations, they are seen as different. For example, a person who scavenges in dustbins and hoards rubbish in their home may be seen as abnormal. But to suggest that behaving in a way that deviates from social norms defines abnormality has limitations:

- This definition could be used to discriminate against people who the majority disapprove of and want to remove from society. For example, in the UK in the early part of the twentieth century, unmarried girls who became pregnant could be diagnosed as mentally ill and locked in asylums.
- Whether behaviour is seen as normal depends on its context. Preaching a sermon is seen as normal in a church, but preaching a sermon in a supermarket might be considered abnormal.
- Social norms and attitudes change. Homosexuality was believed to be a mental illness until the 1970s but is not seen as such today.
- Social norms vary within and between cultures; there is not one universally acceptable set of social norms. In Muslim countries, a woman who dressed provocatively in public would be viewed as socially deviant, but this behaviour is common among women in Western society.

Item 3
Abnormality as failure to function adequately

People who cannot look after themselves, or who are perceived to be irrational or out of control, are often viewed as abnormal. The problem with this is that it involves others in making value judgements about what it means to function adequately. The individuals themselves may not think they

have a problem and their unusual behaviour may be a way of coping with their difficulties in life.

Item 4
Abnormality as deviation from ideal mental health

Jahoda (1958) identified six conditions associated with ideal mental health:

1 a positive self-attitude and high self-esteem
2 a drive to realise self-potential (personal growth)
3 the ability to cope with stress
4 being in control and making your own decisions (personal autonomy)
5 an accurate perception of reality and the ability to feel for others
6 the ability to adapt to changes in one's environment

This approach also has limitations:

- The degree to which a person meets the six criteria may vary over time. Thus, the degree to which any individual can be defined as 'normal' might vary from day to day.
- It is a subjective standard — it is difficult to measure self-esteem and self-potential.
- It is an ethnocentric standard — it describes normality from an individualistic culture rather than from a collectivist culture.
- By this standard, it is possible that most people could be defined as abnormal.

Item 5
Cultural relativism in definitions of abnormality

A 'culture' is not a group of people but the customs and attitudes that a group of people share. A 'sub-culture' is a group within a society which share some practices with the dominant culture but which also has some special attitudes and customs.

Cultural relativism means that we cannot judge normality or abnormality without reference to the norms of the culture where the behaviour arose. Behaviour that may appear abnormal in one cultural setting, because it deviates from the norms of that culture, is not abnormal in its native cultural setting. Definitions of abnormality are limited because they are culturally specific.

A psychological abnormality can be said to be:
- **Absolute** — if the disorder occurs with the same symptoms and with the same frequency in all cultures. This is probably true for schizophrenia.
- **Universal** — the disorder occurs in all cultures but not with the same frequency. This is true for some disorders, such as depression, which is more common, for example, in urban and industrial societies.
- **Culturally-relative** — the disorder is unique (or almost unique) to particular cultures and only meaningful within those cultures. These are called **culture-bound syndromes**.

Because cultures differ in their attitudes and customs, it is not possible to formulate absolute definitions of abnormality. In the Trobriand Islands, it is normal for a son to clean the bones of his dead father and to give them to relatives to wear. It would be seen as abnormal for a widow not to wear the bones of her late husband. In the UK, this behaviour would be seen as abnormal, though in the Victorian age it was quite normal for a widow to wear rings and brooches woven from the hair of her deceased husband.

Topic 1 Defining psychological abnormality

Answers

1 Read your textbook and Items 1–4.

1a

  a Outline the main assumption of the statistical infrequency definition of abnormality.

b

  b Describe the deviation from social norms definition of abnormality.

  c How have psychologists defined ideal mental health?

c

  d Explain *one* limitation of the statistical infrequency definition of abnormality.

d

  e Explain *one* limitation of the deviation from social norms definition of abnormality.

e

  f Give *one* reason why the definition of abnormality as a 'failure to function adequately' is not useful.

f

2 Read your textbook and Item 5.

  a Explain what is meant by 'cultural relativism'.

  b Outline why cultural relativism is a limitation of the statistical infrequency definition of abnormality.

  c Outline why cultural relativism is a limitation of the deviation from social norms definition of abnormality

  d Outline why cultural relativism is a limitation of the deviation from the ideal mental health definition of abnormality

  e Outline how psychologists could find out whether any psychological abnormality, such as depressive illness, is a universal phenomenon.

  f What is a psychological abnormality called if it occurs only in a specific culture?

2a

b

c

d

e

f

Topic 2 Models of abnormality

Research into individual differences involves looking at how genetics and the environment affect our development. Biological approaches to abnormality explore differences caused by genetics, biochemistry and brain anatomy. Psychological approaches to abnormality look at how early childhood experiences, family systems and the unconscious mind affect the way people behave, and how individuals differ in how they think about themselves and the world. Behaviourist approaches look at how the consequences of behaviour reinforce abnormal behaviour and thinking patterns.

This topic focuses on models of abnormality and the assumptions made by biological and psychological (including psychodynamic, behavioural and cognitive) models in their perspectives on the causes and treatment of abnormality.

Item 1
The biological model

The biological model assumes that psychological abnormalities are symptoms of underlying physical causes. Thus, psychological disorders may be referred to as 'mental illnesses'. These are seen as arising from:

- **Genetics.** This is evidenced by the fact that some mental disorders, such as schizophrenia, run in families, suggesting an underlying genetic abnormality.
- **Infection.** Abnormalities may be caused by infection.

General paresis is a condition involving mood swings and delusions and, eventually, paralysis and death. This is caused by syphilis and can now be treated with drugs.

- **Neurotransmitters.** These are biochemicals that carry the signals between brain cells. Too much or too little neurotransmitter may result in psychological disorders. For example, too much dopamine is thought to lead to schizophrenia.
- **Brain injury.** Patients who have suffered a stroke, particularly when the stroke damage is centred in the left hemisphere (in right-handed people), may lose their ability to understand and/or produce speech. Phineas Gage was a construction worker in the 1800s in America. As a result of an explosion, an iron rod penetrated his brain and destroyed part of his frontal lobes. He survived but it was reported that his personality had changed and that he had become disorganised and impulsive.

Treatments based on the biological model of abnormality

Treatments in this model assume that psychological abnormalities are symptoms of underlying physical causes.

- **Drug therapies (chemotherapy).** Anti-anxiety drugs, such as benzodiazepines, can be used to relieve tension. Anti-psychotic drugs can be used to reduce mental confusion and delusions. Anti-depressant drugs, such as Prozac, can be used to elevate mood. These treatments assume that an imbalance in biochemistry (neurotransmitters) is the cause of the abnormality.

- **Electroconvulsive therapy (ECT)** is an electric shock passed through the temporal lobes of the brain to produce cortical seizure and convulsions. ECT is still used to treat severe cases of depression, but this therapy has declined in use since the 1970s.
- **Psychosurgery** means literally cutting away parts of the brain (e.g. lobotomy). President John Kennedy's sister Rosemary suffered from epilepsy. Her father gave his consent for her to have psychosurgery, but afterwards she was brain damaged and was permanently confined to an institution. This treatment assumes that part of the brain is injured or is malfunctioning and that if the malfunctioning part is removed, the cause of the abnormality will be gone. Psychosurgery is a 'last resort' treatment for epilepsy. Roger Sperry was awarded the Nobel prize for physiology or medicine for his 'split brain studies'. He studied patients who had had their corpus-callosum severed because they suffered from severe epilepsy.

Evaluation of the biological model
Strengths
- The model does not blame people for their abnormal behaviour. It has led to a more humane treatment of the mentally ill (better than burning at the stake).
- The scientific status and association with the medical profession means that this model enjoys credibility.
- Objective evidence shows that biological causes can be linked to psychological symptoms, e.g. dopamine levels in schizophrenia.

Limitations
- Psychiatrists such as Szasz and Laing object to the medical model. They see the use of labels, such as 'mentally ill', as a way of pathologising people whose behaviour we do not like or cannot explain.
- There may be problems of validity and reliability in diagnosing the type of abnormality. There is frequently a degree of overlap between symptoms of different disorders, meaning the diagnosis may be unreliable.
- The model takes a reductionist approach to psychological abnormality and ignores the relationship between the mind and body.

Evaluation of biological therapies
Advantages
- It is claimed that biological therapies (drugs) reduce the symptoms of conditions, such as schizophrenia, that could formerly not be treated.
- Drug therapy can be used alongside therapies based on psychological approaches.
- Drug treatments are easy to administer and do not involve the patient changing their lifestyle or behaviour.

Limitations
- Biological therapies may cause ethical concerns. Some drug therapies can have unpleasant side effects. Patients with some conditions may be unable to understand the implications of their treatment and thus be unable to give their informed consent.
- Taking drugs may lead to addiction and dependency.
- Drugs may simply suppress the symptoms, not cure the disorder. The use of drugs may divert attention away from the real causes of the problem.
- Drug treatments take a reductionist approach to the treatment of abnormality because they ignore psychosocial factors.

Item 2
The behaviourist model of psychological abnormality

The behaviourist model makes three assumptions. First, it assumes that all behaviour is learned; second, that what has been learned can be unlearned; and third, that abnormal behaviour is learned in the same way as normal behaviour. This model sees the abnormal behaviour as the problem and not a symptom of an underlying cause.

Behaviourists propose that **classical conditioning** can explain phobias. In classical conditioning, an unconditioned stimulus, such as an unexpected loud noise, triggers a natural reflex, e.g. the startle response and fear. But, if another stimulus, e.g. seeing a spider, occurs at the same time, this may in future elicit the fear response. Watson and Rayner (1920) demonstrated how classical conditioning could explain the way in which fear could be learned.

Behaviourists also propose that abnormal behaviour can be learned by the process of **operant conditioning**, in which behaviour is learned through the consequences of our actions. If our actions result in rewarding consequences (positive reinforcement), or in something nasty ceasing (negative reinforcement), we will repeat the behaviour, but we will not repeat behaviour that has bad outcomes. Phobias such as fear of heights can be learned in this way. We become anxious at the thought of climbing the ladder, so we employ a window cleaner in order to avoid using a ladder, and this removes the anxiety (negative reinforcement).

Treatments based on the behaviourist model of abnormality

The treatments proposed by the behaviourist model are based on the assumption that abnormal behaviour is learned in the same way as normal behaviour and that it can be unlearned. Abnormal behaviour is seen as a 'problem to be cured'.

Behaviourists try to identify the **reinforcers** of abnormal behaviour and change the consequences of behaviour. Behavioural therapies may use classical conditioning in which an undesirable behaviour can be paired with an unpleasant response (aversion therapy). Or they may use **systematic desensitisation** in which phobics can be gradually reintroduced to a feared object or situation. Token economies, based on operant conditioning, are often used in schools and hospitals to change the behaviour of delinquents and anorexics. In token economies, clients earn small rewards (reinforcers) for desirable behaviour, and the small rewards (tokens) can be collected up and exchanged for larger rewards (secondary reinforcers).

Evaluation of the behaviourist model and therapies
Strengths

- The model proposes a simple testable explanation that is supported by experimental evidence.
- Behaviourist therapies are effective for treating phobias, obsessive compulsive disorders and eating disorders, and are appropriate for those whose symptoms are behavioural.
- The behavioural model is hopeful as it predicts that people can change (re-learn) their behaviour.

Limitations

- The model is criticised as being dehumanising and mechanistic (Heather 1976). People are reduced to programmed stimulus-response units.
- Token economies involving reinforcers that withhold a basic human right, such as food, clothing or privacy, are unethical. These procedures have been ruled illegal in the USA.
- The model cannot explain all psychological disorders. Conditioning cannot cure all disorders, e.g. schizophrenia.

Item 3
The psychodynamic model of psychological abnormality

The psychodynamic model, based on Freudian theory, assumes that behaviour is motivated by unconscious forces, and that abnormal behaviour has its origins in unresolved, unconscious conflicts in early childhood. The model is based on Freud's proposal that the human personality comprises the id, the ego and the superego, and that the **development of the personality progresses in five psychosexual stages** (the oral, anal, phallic, latent and genital stages). According to the psychodynamic model, in childhood the ego is not fully developed, and is thus unable to manage the conflicting demands of the id and the superego. Conflict and anxiety may result and the ego defends itself by repression, projection or displacement. In repression, anxiety is hidden (repressed) into the unconscious, but stress in adulthood may trigger the repressed conflict, leading to psychological abnormality.

Treatments based on the psychodynamic model of abnormality

This model assumes that behaviour is motivated by unconscious forces and treatments are focused on three objectives: first, to free healthy impulses; second, to strengthen and re-educate the ego; and third, to change the superego so that it causes less anxiety. This is achieved by **psychoanalysis**, during which dream analysis and free association may be used. In **free association**, based on the idea that the ego will try to repress unacceptable impulses, the therapist interprets pauses or hesitations when talking about certain topics as signs of repressed anxiety. In **dream analysis**, based on Freud's proposal that dreams represent unconscious wish-fulfilment, the therapist interprets dreams as symbols of repressed wishes. By using **thematic apperception tests**, the client may reveal unconscious thoughts which the therapist interprets. In the **process of transference**, the client transfers repressed conflicts onto the therapist who 'becomes the parent' the child lacked or needed to resolve the unconscious conflict.

Evaluation of the psychodynamic model and therapies
Strengths

- The model identifies the importance of traumatic childhood experience in adult problems.
- Freud's theories changed people's attitudes to mental illness, and psychosomatic illnesses demonstrate the link between mind and body.
- The model does not hold people responsible for their behaviour as the causes of behaviour are unconscious.

Limitations

- The model is not scientific; Freud's theories are not falsifiable (his hypotheses are not testable).
- The model overemphasises past experience, when clients' problems may have causes in the 'here and now'.
- Eysenck (1952) found that 66% of patients in therapy recover within 2 years, but so do 66% of patients who have no therapy.
- Psychoanalysis may only benefit certain clients — the young, attractive, verbal, intelligent and successful (the YAVIS model) — and are more likely to be effective with clients who have a positive attitude (belief) towards therapy (a self-fulfilling prophesy).
- The model is reductionist and ignores biological and socio-cultural factors.

Item 4
The cognitive model of psychological abnormality

The cognitive model of abnormality is based on the assumption that the human mind is like an information processor and that people can control how they select, store and think about information. The cognitive model proposes that to be normal is to be able to use cognitive processes to monitor and control our behaviour, and that abnormal behaviour is caused by faulty or irrational thoughts. In the cognitive model, psychological problems are caused when people make incorrect inferences about themselves or others, and have negative thoughts about themselves and the future. **Beck and Clark (1988)** found that irrational beliefs were common in patients suffering anxiety and depression. For example, depressive people often believe that they are unloved, that they are failures as parents, and that nothing good will ever happen in the future.

Treatments based on the cognitive model of abnormality

Treatments based on this model focus on helping the patient change irrational or negative thoughts to ones that are rational and positive. The objective of treatment is to correct, by **cognitive restructuring**, unrealistic ideas, so that thinking becomes an effective means of controlling behaviour. The therapist supports the patient through a process of cognitive behaviour therapy (CBT) until thought processes become more rational. Examples of treatments based on the cognitive model are rational emotive therapy for depression (Beck 1976) and stress inoculation training (Meichenbaum).

Evaluation of the cognitive model and therapies
Strengths

- The model focuses on how the individual experiences the world and his or her feelings and beliefs rather than relying on interpretations by other people.
- The model is hopeful as it assumes people have the power to change their behaviour.
- Cognitive-based therapies may increase self-efficacy and self-belief and thus improve people's lives in the future.
- Supporting evidence from Hollon et al. (1992) found CBT was more effective than drugs for treating depression and anxiety.

Limitations

- The model may encourage the idea that people are responsible for their own psychological problems, i.e. that they could be 'normal' if they so chose. This could lead to people being blamed for psychological abnormalities.

- Treatments may only be effective for people who have good problem-solving skills, an insight into their behaviour and the willingness to spend time on 'the problem'.
- Treatments may only be effective for anxiety disorders and depressive illnesses. They may not be generalisable to many psychological abnormalities.
- The model is reductionist as it ignores biological causes of psychological abnormality such as genetics or biochemistry.

Item 5
Three hypothetical case studies

1 Janus suffers from severe anxiety and has frequent panic attacks. He has been diagnosed as having an anxiety disorder.

2 Hector has been anxious and depressed since he became unemployed. He feels useless and knows he will never get another job.

3 Pandora has a severe snake phobia. She refuses to go on holiday with her family in case she sees a snake.

Topic 2 Models of abnormality

Answers

1 Read your textbook and Item 1.

a Outline *two* assumptions of the biological approach to psychological abnormality.

1a

b Your friend is diagnosed as suffering from a depressive illness. Explain how a biological psychologist might explain his or her illness.

b

c Outline *one* assumption of the biological model of abnormality in relation to its views on the treatment of abnormality.

c

d Describe *one* strength and *one* limitation of the biological model of abnormality. Write two sentences and link them with the word 'however'.

d

e Describe *one* advantage and *one* limitation of the use of drugs in the treatment of psychological abnormalities. Write two sentences and link them with the phrase 'on the other hand'.

e

2 Read your textbook and Item 2.

  a Outline *two* assumptions of the behaviourist approach to psychological abnormality.

  b Identify *two* processes that, according to the behaviourist model, may cause psychological abnormality.

  c Your friend is diagnosed as suffering from a depressive illness. Explain how a behaviourist psychologist might explain his or her illness.

  d Describe *one* strength and *one* limitation of the behaviourist model of abnormality.

  e Describe *one* advantage and *one* limitation of the use of behaviour therapies to treat psychological abnormalities.

2a

b

c

d

e

Topic 2 Models of abnormality

3 Read your textbook and Item 3.

a Outline *two* assumptions of the psycho-dynamic approach to psychological abnormality.

b Identify *two* factors that, according to the psychodynamic model, may cause psychological abnormality.

c Your friend is diagnosed as suffering from a depressive illness. Explain the assumptions made by a psychoanalyst when explaining his or her illness.

d Describe *one* method of treatment that is associated with the psychodynamic model.

e Describe *two* strengths of the psycho-dynamic model of abnormality.

f You are a well-known psychoanalyst and you have been asked to write a magazine article describing 'the charac-teristics of people who will benefit from psychoanalysis'. From what you have learned about the psychodynamic model of abnormality, describe the 'ideal patient'.
(**Hint:** don't describe the illness; describe the *characteristics* of the patient.)

g Describe *two* limitations of the psychodynamic model of psychological abnormalities.

3a

b

c

d

e

f

g

4 Read your textbook and Item 4.

a Outline *two* assumptions of the cognitive approach to psychological abnormality.

b Identify *two* factors that, according to the cognitive model, may cause psychological abnormality.

c Your friend is diagnosed as suffering from a depressive illness. Describe the assumptions of the cognitive model of psychological abnormality and how this model explains depression.

d Describe *one* method of treatment that is associated with the cognitive model.

e In two sentences, describe *one* strength and *one* limitation of the cognitive model of abnormality. Start the second sentence with the word 'however'.

f In two sentences, describe *one* advantage and *one* limitation of using cognitive restructuring therapies to treat psychological abnormalities. Start the second sentence with the words 'on the other hand'.

4a

b

c

d

e

f

Topic 2 Models of abnormality

5 Read your textbook and Items 1–5. For *each* hypothetical case below, describe the assumptions of either the biological model or any *one* psychological model of abnormality as to possible causes of the problem.

Janus suffers from severe anxiety and has frequent panic attacks. He has been diagnosed as having an anxiety disorder.

Hector has been anxious and depressed since he became unemployed. He feels useless and knows he will never get another job.

Pandora has a severe snake phobia. She refuses to go on holiday with her family in case she sees a snake.

5

Assumptions of biological model	Assumptions of psychological model
Janus	
Hector	
Pandora	

6 *Exam practice*

Review your notes and Items 1–4. Outline the biological model of abnormality and consider whether it can adequately explain psychological abnormality.

a Write a list of points as an outline plan for this essay.

b In the exam you should describe, in about 100 words, appropriate psychological evidence (AO1 skills), and then provide about 200 words of evaluative commentary (AO2 skills).

c Try to use one of these phrases for each evaluation point you list:
- One strength of this research is…
- On the other hand…
- This implies that…
- This is useful because…
- Not all psychologists agree, for example…
- There are advantages to X because…
- These findings are reliable/unreliable because…

d In your outline, identify the psychological evidence you will use and the evaluative points you will need.

An eating disorder is an abnormal relationship with food. The abnormality may be severe under-eating (anorexia nervosa), bingeing and purging (bulimia nervosa) or over-eating (obesity). Eating disorders are examples of psychological abnormality. This topic focuses on psychological research into eating disorders, including the clinical characteristics of anorexia nervosa and bulimia nervosa and explanations of these disorders in terms of models of abnormality.

- Lack of control over eating and bingeing
- Fluctuating body weight but usually within 10% of normal weight
- Self-image dependent on body shape
- Onset usually around the age of 20
- Fifty per cent more common in females
- May involve purging by self-induced vomiting and/or use of laxatives

Item 1
The characteristics of anorexia nervosa and bulimia nervosa

Anorexia nervosa
- Intense fear of becoming fat despite being underweight
- Body weight less than 85% of expected weight
- Distorted thinking about body shape and weight
- Amenorrhoea (absence of menstruation) for more than three cycles
- Onset usually in adolescence
- Ninety per cent of cases are female
- More frequent in middle-class females
- Five per cent death rate

Bulimia nervosa
- Episodes of binge eating — huge amounts of food eaten in a short period of time
- Bingeing occurs more than twice a week over an extended period of time

Item 2
The biological model of anorexia nervosa and bulimia nervosa

The biological model of anorexia nervosa and bulimia nervosa explains the causes in terms of physiological factors, such as genetics and biochemistry (abnormal levels of neuro-transmitters).

Holland et al. (1988): genetic vulnerability to anorexia nervosa

Aim To investigate whether there was a higher concordance rate of anorexia nervosa in monozygotic twins (MZ) than in dizygotic twins (DZ). MZ twins are genetically identical, whereas DZ twins share only 50% of the same genes. If there is a genetic basis for anorexia, it was therefore expected that a higher concordance rate for anorexia would be found in identical twins.

Procedures Thirty-five sets of twins, in which one twin had anorexia, were interviewed and questioned about their eating habits, whether any of their relatives had an eating disorder and how satisfied they were with their body shape.

Findings Of 30 female twin pairs, 16 were identical and 14 were non-identical. Of the identical twins, 56% both suffered from anorexia, but of the non-identical twins, only 7% both suffered. For both identical and non-identical twins, in comparison to the population, there was an increase in the incidence of anorexia among their relatives. None of the four male anorexics had a twin having anorexia.

Conclusion The increased incidence of anorexia among identical twins suggests there may be a genetic vulnerability for anorexia nervosa, but that the condition may be triggered by environmental conditions.

Criticism Because identical twins are treated more simi-larly than non-identical twins, and may also imitate each other, it is possible that the increased incidence of anorexia among identical twins can be explained by environmental factors. Generalisation may require caution as this was a small sample.

Kendler et al. (1991): genetic vulnerability to bulimia nervosa

Aim To replicate the Holland et al. study, looking at genetic vulnerability to bulimia nervosa by studying twins.

Procedures The study interviewed 2163 female twins in a similar way to Holland et al.

Findings A 23% concordance rate (both twins bulimic) in the MZ twins compared to 9% concordance rate in the DZ twins.

Conclusion These findings support the suggestion of a genetic vulnerability for bulimia nervosa, but the percentage concordance suggests that genes are not wholly responsible, and that predisposition to the disorder is triggered by some environmental factor(s).

Criticism Because identical twins are treated more similarly than non-identical twins, and may also imitate each other, it is possible that the increased incidence of bulimia in iden-tical twins can be explained by environmental factors. If the explanation were wholly genetic, the concordance rate in MZ twins would be expected to be 100% as their genes are iden-tical. This was a large sample but only 58 twins reported symptoms of bulimia. Biological explanations cannot explain the increase in eating disorders in the last 20 years.

Fava et al. (1989): neurotransmitters as a factor in anorexia and bulimia

Findings The study found links between anorexia and bulimia and changes in levels of serotonin and noradrenaline in the brain. Eating large amounts of carbohydrates increases serotonin levels which has a positive effect on mood. Bulimics have been found to have low levels of serotonin. Fava suggested that this underlying biological cause may explain the bingeing behaviour characteristic of bulimia nervosa.

Criticisms It is difficult to establish the direction of the relationship between low levels of serotonin and bulimia; the bingeing and purging could be the cause of the low levels of serotonin. In addition, bulimics do not only binge on foods that are high in carbohydrates. In support of this theory, anti-depressant drugs, especially selective serotonin re-uptake indicators (SSRIs), have been found to be an effective treatment for some people with bulimia.

Item 3
Explanations of anorexia and bulimia: the psychodynamic model

One approach within the psychodynamic theory suggests that anorexics stop eating in order to avoid developing an adult body shape and thus the anxiety associated with sexual maturity. Another psychodynamic approach associates eating disorders with the struggle for autonomy and with dysfunctional families.

Family systems theory proposes that the culture within the family can be linked to the development of anorexia. Family systems theorists Minuchin et al. (1975) argue that eating disorders are caused, at least partly, by distinctive patterns of interaction within families. In general, family theorists regard eating disorders as symptoms of a family's difficulty in allowing an adolescent daughter to separate and individuate. The eating disorder becomes a means for the daughter to express the family's conflict over her separation. The girl asserts herself by not eating while, at the same time, her starvation holds her back from development into autonomous womanhood. However, family conflict may be the result of living with an anorexic child. The family systems theory cannot explain the huge increase in eating disorders in recent years, nor can it explain why boys develop eating disorders.

Bruch (1971): a psychodynamic explanation of anorexia

Bruch suggested that anorexia is a response to poor parenting and is a way of exerting control. In the study, 55 female and 9 male anorexics were psychoanalysed. Bruch concluded that individuals with anorexia nervosa are in conflict with their parents, particularly their mother, and they struggle to gain a sense of identity and autonomy. The characteristic of the mothers was that they did not provide appropriate responses to their children's needs. For example, mothers provided food at the 'correct meal times', not when the child said he or she was hungry. This led to the child being unable to distinguish between their internal needs and their emotions.

Criticism This theory depends upon the therapist's interpretation of what is said during analysis and is difficult to test. The anorexic may agree with the therapist's interpretation because she seeks approval (social desirability bias). In addition, case studies are unique and the findings cannot be generalised to others. In support of this theory, Halmi (1995) found that bulimics were unable to distinguish hunger from emotions and that when they were angry or upset they believed they were hungry.

Item 4
Explanations of anorexia and bulimia: the behaviourist model

The behaviourist approach assumes eating disorders are learned through classical and/or operant conditioning or modelling. **Leitenberg et al. (1968)** suggest that both classical and operant conditioning are involved in eating disorders. In anorexia, eating may be associated with anxiety because eating too much leads to weight gain. Thus avoiding eating reduces anxiety. The resultant weight loss also reduces anxiety and acts as a positive reinforcement of the not-eating behaviour.

The reinforcement cycle in anorexia (operant conditioning)
- Stage 1 — achieve weight loss
- Stage 2 — receive praise and admiration for weight loss
- Stage 3 — feel good about self and wish to lose more weight
- Stage 4 — weight loss becomes associated with praise from others and feeling good

The reinforcement cycle in bulimia (classical conditioning)
Eating is associated with anxiety; thus weight loss and refusal of food reduces anxiety.
- Stage 1 — bingeing causes anxiety
- Stage 2 — vomiting reduces anxiety
- Stage 3 — vomiting (a reflex behaviour) is now associated with the reduction of anxiety

Evaluation
Hallstein (1965) used behavioural therapies to treat bulimia by rewarding clients for maintaining body weight. But this theory cannot account for individual differences in vulnerability to eating disorders, nor why there is not an equal distribution of eating disorders across all cultures.

Item 5
How social learning theory explains anorexia and bulimia

An alternative behaviourist approach focuses on social learning theory and modelling. Social learning theorists propose that in Western culture:
- the ideal woman is slim
- slim women are rewarded by attention
- young women copy those they identify with and admire

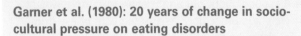

Garner et al. (1980): 20 years of change in socio-cultural pressure on eating disorders

Aim To use magazine photographs and articles to test whether attitudes to female body shapes changed between 1959 and 1978.

Procedures Centrefolds from *Playboy* magazine and pictures of contestants and winners of the Miss America contest in the years 1959 to 1978 were studied, as well as articles on dieting in six popular women's magazines.

Findings The photographs showed a change in the preferred shape for women. Bust and hip sizes became smaller and shape became thinner and more angular. Sixty-nine percent of the *Playboy* centrefolds and 60% of the Miss America participants weighed 15% below the average weights for their height and age over the period. Although the average female weight had increased in the 1970s, the winning contestants weighed significantly less than the other contestants. In the magazines, the number of articles on diet increased.

Conclusion Changing social pressures and family expectations have an impact on the development of eating disorders.

Criticisms The study has high ecological validity — these were real publications. However, even though the study shows a correlational relationship, it cannot prove that the mass media cause eating disorders. Millions are exposed to images of thin women in the media, and most do not develop eating disorders, so this theory cannot explain individual differences.

Field et al. (1999): the effect of the mass media

Aim To determine the extent of peer and media influence on the development of bulimia nervosa.

Procedures In a repeated measures study, 7000 adolescent girls aged 9–14 were asked to complete questionnaires. Questions were asked about vomiting and laxative use, the importance of thinness to peers, their desire to look like females portrayed in the media and the development of sexual characteristics. A year later, the same girls were asked to complete the same questionnaire.

Findings Seventy-four girls reported that they had begun to use vomiting and/or laxatives to control their weight. Purging was significantly correlated with (a) the development of pubic hair, (b) the importance of thinness to peers and (c) desire to look like media role models.

Conclusion Both media and peer groups influence the desire to control weight in girls. The study recommended that the mass media should employ more role models who are not underweight.

Evaluation of social learning explanations of eating disorders

Since all women are exposed to similar role models, the social learning explanation does not explain why some develop eating disorders while others do not. However, this approach may help us understand why there has been an increase in such disorders in recent years and why females are more likely to develop them.

(**Note:** it might be a useful exercise to compare the body shapes of film actresses in 'old' films to the body shapes of film actresses in contemporary films. Have role models continued to get thinner since the 1970s?)

Item 6
Cross-cultural research into eating disorders

Cross-cultural studies of eating disorders suggest that anorexia is not always associated with social attitudes about fat or the body.

Hsu (1996) concluded that dieting is a major risk factor for the development of an eating disorder, and that the prevalence of eating disorders appears to increase in proportion to the prevalence of dieting behaviour. However, Hsu found that anorexic patients in Hong Kong and Singapore denied being phobic about getting fat and gave other explanations for their self-starvation. Hsu theorises that bulimic patterns of disordered eating may be explained by social pressures, and that without the cultural emphasis on thinness, the incidence of bulimia would not be so great. In the case of anorexia nervosa, other psychological factors may be more important.

Garner et al. (1980) looked at 55 female ballet students between the ages of 11 and 14 in Toronto and found 25.7% incidence of anorexia, 2.9% incidence of bulimia and 11.4% partial symptoms of anorexia or bulimia — far higher than in the general population. This supports the theory that in cultures where thinness is the valued norm, eating disorders increase.

Lee, Hsu and Wing (1992) found that bulimia was non-existent in Chinese girls in Hong Kong. In China, obesity is rare, dieting is uncommon, and being told that you have gained weight is a compliment. They also noted that bulimia was rare in Chinese populations in Singapore, Malaysia and Hong Kong where obesity is rare and where success for a woman is not linked to physical appearance.

Item 7
Explanations of anorexia and bulimia: the cognitive model

The cognitive approach focuses on the way people think about their body shape and their weight and proposes that people with eating disorders have distorted views (cognitive biases) about their body shape and weight.

Garfinkel and Garner (1982) assessed anorexics' perceptions of their body size. They found that anorexics overestimated their body size and that this overestimation was greater than in control groups.

Cooper and Taylor (1988) found that, although people with bulimia are usually not overweight, they have distorted beliefs and perceive the discrepancy between their 'ideal' and actual body size as larger than it is. This is because their desired body size is smaller than that of most people and because they overestimate their actual body size.

Fallon and Rozin (1985) asked males and female participants to indicate their ideal body size and the body size that

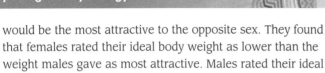

would be the most attractive to the opposite sex. They found that females rated their ideal body weight as lower than the weight males gave as most attractive. Males rated their ideal body weight as higher than the weight women found most attractive.

Evaluation of cognitive explanations of eating disorders

It is difficult to find out whether cognitive biases and distorted thinking are the causes of eating disorders or the result. If biased thinking (overestimating of body size) existed before the onset of the eating disorder, then this may explain its development. If the biased thinking is the result of the eating disorder, then cognitive behavioural therapy to help people perceive their body in a more rational way will have no effect on the underlying eating disorder.

Item 8
The case conference

A conference has been convened to discuss the case of Marie Celeste. Ms Celeste is 19, the only daughter of a famous ballet dancer, and although she is 1.75 m (5' 9") tall she only weighs 37 kg (less than 6 stones). She has anorexia nervosa. At the meeting are four eminent psychologists. All the psychologists conduct research into eating disorders, but each takes a different approach. Dr Gene takes the biological approach, Dr Freud favours the psychodynamic approach, Dr Sun takes the social learning approach and Dr Cogito favours the cognitive approach.

1 Read your textbook and Item 1.

a What is meant by the term 'eating disorder'?

b The items listed in the table are characteristics of anorexia nervosa and bulimia nervosa. Circle anorexia or bulimia or both for each one.

1a

b

• Intense fear of becoming fat despite being underweight	ANOREXIA	BULIMIA
• Bingeing occurs more than twice a week over an extended period of time	ANOREXIA	BULIMIA
• May involve purging by self-induced vomiting and/or use of laxatives	ANOREXIA	BULIMIA
• Body weight less than 85% of expected weight	ANOREXIA	BULIMIA
• Onset usually around the age of 20	ANOREXIA	BULIMIA
• Fifty per cent more common in females	ANOREXIA	BULIMIA
• Distorted thinking about body shape and weight	ANOREXIA	BULIMIA
• Lack of control over eating and bingeing	ANOREXIA	BULIMIA
• Absence of menstruation for more than three cycles	ANOREXIA	BULIMIA
• Fluctuating body weight but usually within 10% of normal weight	ANOREXIA	BULIMIA
• Onset usually in adolescence	ANOREXIA	BULIMIA
• Ninety per cent of cases are females	ANOREXIA	BULIMIA
• Episodes of binge eating	ANOREXIA	BULIMIA

c Describe *two* differences in the clinical characteristics of anorexia nervosa and bulimia nervosa.

c

Topic 3 Critical issue: eating disorders

2 Read your textbook and Item 2.

a Outline how the biological model of psychological abnormality explains eating disorders.

2a

b Outline the procedures and findings of *one* study into the biological causes of anorexia nervosa.

b

c Outline the procedures and findings of *one* study into the biological causes of bulimia nervosa.

c

d Give *two* criticisms of the biological explanation of anorexia nervosa.

d

3 Read your textbook and Item 3.

a Describe *one* psychodynamic explanation of eating disorders.

b Describe the procedures and conclusions of *one* study taking the psychodynamic approach to anorexia nervosa.

b

c Explain *one* limitation of the psycho-dynamic approach to eating disorders.

c

Topic 3 Critical issue: eating disorders

4 Read your textbook and Item 4.
 a Outline how the behaviourist model of psychological abnormality explains eating disorders.

4a

 b Explain how reinforcement of behaviour may contribute to the development of anorexia.

b

 c In two sentences, explain *one* strength and *one* limitation of the behaviourist theory that bulimia nervosa is learned behaviour. Start the second paragraph with the word 'however'.

c

 d Suggest how a behaviourist psychologist might use a token economy as a treatment for a client with anorexia nervosa.

d

5 Read your textbook and Item 5.

  a Outline how social learning theorists explain the development of an eating disorder.

  b Describe the aims, procedures and findings of *one* study that looked at how images in the mass media may be related to the development of eating disorders.

  c Describe *one* strength and *one* limitation of the study you described in **b** above.

  d 'The incidence of eating disorders is increasing.' With reference to psychological research, explain how the social learning theory of eating disorders accounts for this increase.

  e Outline *one* limitation of the suggestion that images of 'underweight role models' in the mass media cause women to develop eating disorders.

5a

b Aims

Procedures

Findings

c

d

e

6 Read your textbook and Items 5 and 6, and revise Item 2 in Topic 1.

a Describe how social norms may be related to the development of eating disorders.

6a

b Explain how cross-cultural research supports the theory that the development of an eating disorder results from pressure to 'fit in' with social norms.

b

c Explain whether you would describe an eating disorder as a psychological abnormality that is absolute, universal or culturally relative.

c

7 Read your textbook and Item 7.

  a Outline how the cognitive model of psychological abnormality explains eating disorders.

  b Outline psychological evidence that suggests irrational thinking is associated with an eating disorder.

  c Outline *two* criticisms of the cognitive explanation of anorexia nervosa.

7a

b

c

8 Read your textbook and Items 1–7.
In the table, summarise *one biological* and
one psychological theory for anorexia
nervosa OR bulimia nervosa, including
the psychological research that supports
the explanation and its strengths and
limitations.

8

Explanation for anorexia nervosa/ bulimia nervosa	Research study	Criticisms
Biological theory		
Psychological theory		

9 Read your textbook and Item 8.

  a You are the practice secretary and have been asked to take the minutes of the meeting at which Dr Gene, Dr Freud, Dr Sun and Dr Cogito will discuss the case of Ms Celeste. Each doctor has 5 minutes in which to put forward their explanation as to why Ms Celeste has developed anorexia nervosa. Outline what they are likely to say and identify *one* research study they may use as evidence.

  b List *one* limitation for each of the doctors' explanations.

9a Dr Gene

Dr Freud

Dr Sun

Dr Cogito

b Dr Gene

Dr Freud

Dr Sun

Dr Cogito

Topic 3 Critical issue: eating disorders

10 *Exam practice*

Read your textbook and Items 1–7. Assess the extent to which psychological research supports the view that anorexia nervosa is caused by biological factors.

a Write a list of points as an outline plan for this essay.

b In the exam you should describe, in about 100 words, appropriate psychological evidence (AO1 skills), and then provide about 200 words of evaluative commentary (AO2 skills).

c Try to use one of these phrases for each evaluation point you list:

- One strength of this research is…
- On the other hand…
- This implies that…
- This is useful because…
- Not all psychologists agree, for example…
- There are advantages to X because…
- These findings are reliable/unreliable because…

d In your outline, identify the psychological evidence you will use and the evaluative points you will need.

11 *Exam practice*

Read your textbook and Items 1–7. Assess the extent to which research supports the view that bulimia nervosa is caused by psychological factors.

a Write a list of points as an outline plan for this essay.

b In the exam you should describe, in about 100 words, appropriate psychological evidence (AO1 skills), and then provide about 200 words of evaluative commentary (AO2 skills).

c Try to use one of these phrases for each evaluation point you list:
- One strength of this research is…
- On the other hand…
- This implies that…
- This is useful because…
- Not all psychologists agree, for example…
- There are advantages to X because…
- These findings are reliable/unreliable because…

d In your outline, identify the psychological evidence you will use and the evaluative points you will need.